In Search of the Labyrinth

Dad told Carla and Rob about the Labyrinth.

"No one knows where the Labyrinth is," said Dad, "but some people think it might be near these ruins."

"A legend says that the Minotaur, which was half man and half bull, lived in the Labyrinth," said Dad. "Every year, people were made to go into the Labyrinth. They got lost in the maze and the Minotaur ate them."

"Yuk!" said Carla.

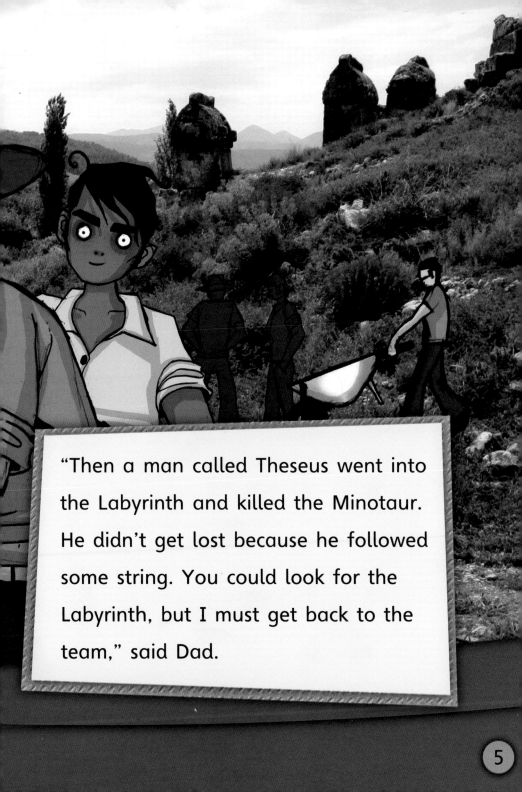

"Then a man called Theseus went into the Labyrinth and killed the Minotaur. He didn't get lost because he followed some string. You could look for the Labyrinth, but I must get back to the team," said Dad.

Carla and Rob saw a tree that had fallen over. It had made a deep hole and there was a dark tunnel.

"I'm going down that tunnel. I might find the Labyrinth," said Rob.

"Don't go down there! You might meet the Minotaur," said Carla.

"Don't be such a baby," said Rob.

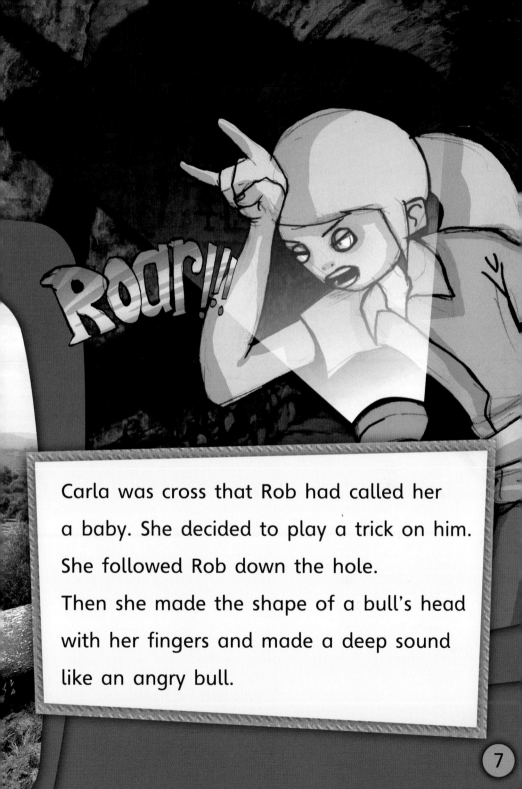

Carla was cross that Rob had called her
a baby. She decided to play a trick on him.
She followed Rob down the hole.
Then she made the shape of a bull's head
with her fingers and made a deep sound
like an angry bull.

Rob looked round and saw the bull's head
on the wall. "It's the Minotaur!" he yelled,
and he ran deeper into the tunnel.
"Come back!" shouted Carla. "It was
only me!" And she ran after him.

At last Carla stopped him.

They looked at the dark tunnels.

"Oh no!" said Rob. "We are lost in the Labyrinth."

Carla was scared. "We'll never find our way out," she said.

But Rob was laughing. "We are not lost," he said. "I played a trick on you. I used some string, just like Theseus. We can follow the string back through the tunnels."

Carla and Rob set off following the string. Just then they heard a deep sound like an angry bull.

"How did you do that?" asked Rob.

"I didn't," said Carla. "I thought you did it."

Carla and Rob looked at each other.
"It must be the Minotaur!" they yelled,
and they raced back through the tunnels
to the tree.

Quiz

Text Detective

- How did Theseus get out of the Labyrinth?
- Why was Carla scared in the Labyrinth?
- Do you think that the Minotaur made the noise at the end of the story?

Word Detective

- **Phonic Assessment:** Vowel phonemes in polysyllabic words
  How many syllables are there in 'going'? What are the vowel phonemes in each syllable? Write the word.
- How many syllables are there in 'about'? What are the vowel phonemes in each syllable? Write the word.
- How many syllables are there in 'follow'? What are the vowel phonemes in each syllable? Write the word.

Super Speller

Can you spell these words from memory?

through   people   angry

HA! HA! HA!

Q What should you do if a bull charges you?

A Pay up quickly!

In this story

 Josh

 Josh's mum

 The housemates

Introduce these tricky words and help the reader when they come across them later!

Tricky words

- brother
- awful
- housemates
- bored
- filthy
- guitar
- programme
- dreamed

Story starter

Josh spends so much time watching TV that he sometimes forgets there are other things he could be doing. One evening he was watching *Kid Big Brother*, a programme where people who don't know one another share a house for a month. The housemates were bored because they had no TV to watch.

Kid Big Brother

Josh was watching *Kid Big Brother* on TV.

"It's awful," he said to his mum. "The housemates don't have a TV to watch!"

"*You* wouldn't like it," said his mum.

"All you ever do is watch TV."

Josh blinked. The TV seemed to be coming closer. He blinked again. No, he was getting closer to the TV. He was being sucked towards the screen! "Mum!" he called. "Help …"

But it was too late – he was sucked right inside the TV.

Josh found himself inside the *Kid Big Brother* house.

"Here's someone new," the housemates said. "Have you brought a TV?"

"No," said Josh.

"We're so bored," they said. "All we can do here is eat and sleep."

"But you can do other things," Josh told them.

"Like what?" they said.

"Like cleaning up this filthy room," said Josh. "There are maggots all over these old burgers!"

"Clean it up yourself," said the housemates. "We're too bored."

So Josh cleaned the room. Then he
looked for some food in the fridge.
"Let's make a snack," he said.
"Make it yourself," the housemates
said. "We're too bored."
So Josh made a snack for himself.

"Why don't we play a game?" said Josh.

"What sort of game?" they asked.

Josh picked up a cricket bat and ball.

"Cricket!" said Josh.

"No way," said the housemates. "We're too bored to play anything."

"You can't just sit there all day saying you're bored!" Josh said.

He picked up a guitar.

"We could play some music," said Josh.

"We can't play the guitar," they said.

"But I can!" cried Josh. "I'll play and you sing!"

"No way," said the housemates. "Singing is too boring."

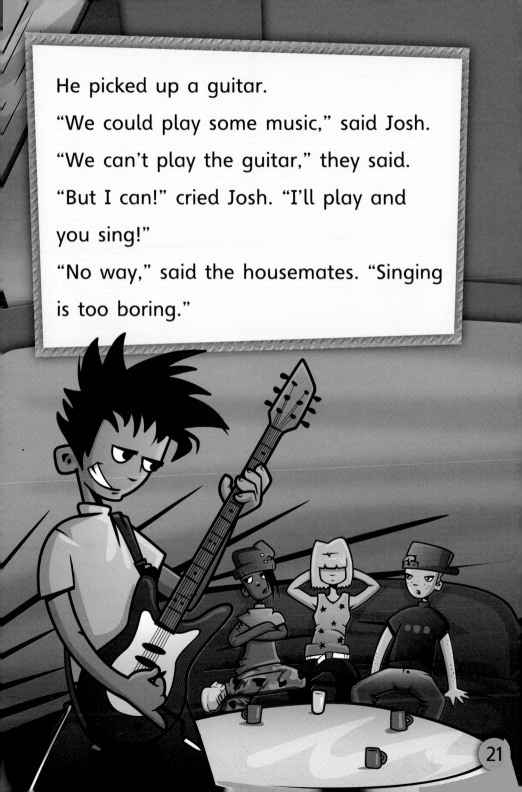

Josh was fed up. "You guys are not just bored, you're very **boring** too! Why would anyone want to watch a TV programme about you?" he said.

Then … **ZAP!** It all went dark. Josh found himself back on his sofa.

"I must have dreamed it," thought Josh. "Those guys were so boring. I really don't want to watch them any more."

He switched off the TV.

"Wow!" laughed his mum. "You just switched off the TV!"

"I did," said Josh. "I **can** do other things, you know!"

23

Quiz

Text Detective

- Why was Josh cross with the housemates?
- What effect did living in the *Kid Big Brother* house have on Josh?
- Would you go on a *Kid Big Brother* programme? Why or why not?

Word Detective

- **Phonic Assessment:** Identifying phonemes in complex words

  How many syllables are there in 'getting'? What are the vowel phonemes in each syllable? Write the word.

- What is the long vowel phoneme in 'would'? Which letters make the long vowel phoneme? Write the word.

- What sound does the 'ed' ending make in 'laughed'? (*d*) Write the word.

Super Speller

Can you spell these words from memory?

someone   found   watch

HA! HA! HA!

Q Why was the boy on the TV?

A Because there was nowhere else to sit!